To Katie

Mary R D Abbind

Catharsis

Mary R. Dobbins

AuthorHouse™
1663 Liberty Drive, Suite 200
Bloomington, IN 47403
www.authorhouse.com
Phone: 1-800-839-8640

© 2009 Mary R. Dobbins. All rights reserved.

No part of this book may be reproduced, stored in a retrieval system, or transmitted by any means without the written permission of the author.

First published by AuthorHouse 3/23/2009

ISBN: 978-1-4389-6781-3 (sc)

Library of Congress Control Number: 2009902569

Printed in the United States of America
Bloomington, Indiana

This book is printed on acid-free paper.

Forward

The following are my thoughts on subjects ranging from love to death, and a few things in between. They include tributes to family and friends; emotions that could not be voiced; and a few smiles along the way.
They are my catharses.
Mary R. Dobbins

Dedication

This book is dedicated to my parents,
Thomas W. and Ruth E. Dobbins.
They taught me to love words and,
from that, poetry.

LOVE

A Little Pup's Love

The brown bitch caught a load of buckshot in the head
    for protecting the body of her dead pup.
She ran and hid under the porch
    of the broken-down pink house.
The man who shot her figured that she was dead;
    he buried the pup and forgot the bitch.
Another pup lived under the porch
    of the old pink house;
He caught grasshoppers and beetles
    and took them under the house to eat.
All through the summer, the man watched
    the thin shepherd pup play.
He tried to catch the pup,
    but it was too fast for the man.
In the late fall, the pup came out to catch food,
    but the man noticed something different,
The pup was looking back toward the porch
    of the pink house.
Slowly, from under the porch
    came the old brown bitch.
She walked slowly at first, nearly falling,
    seeming not to trust the road where she was hurt.
Her face was scarred; patches of hair were gone,
    one half was smaller than the other.
The man saw her and was surprised
    but he understood the reason that she had lived.

A Touch of Fire

So intense it takes
My breath away.
A hand on my arm
To guide the way?

Feelings lost to time.
Or am I mistaken,
Does his touch find
A way to awaken

The fire that once
Burned so bright?
An ember now;
A long dark night.

The touch of his hand
Sent fire to my soul,
Igniting my heart,
But extracting a toll.

Does his touch
Guide the way,
Or will there be
Hell to pay?

Age

Age does not matter
To friends with
Decades of time
They have shared.

Age does not matter
To adults with
Eyes wide open, and
Hearts willing to care.

Age does not matter
Once we have heard
The message that
Our hearts send.

Age does not matter
When lives cross
And we find
A true friend.

Burnt

I once touched
The flame of love.
With wings I flew
And soared above.

Alas, I flew too close,
Like Icarus to the Sun;
The flame too hot,
My flight too soon done.

Burnt by the flame,
Consumed by the heat,
My wax wings melted,
This flight incomplete.

Crashing to the ground
In a burning heap
All I could do
Was sit and weep.

Change of Seasons

Spring brought warmth
To the Earth and
Fire to my soul.

Awakening the flowers
And melting the icy wall
Around my heart.

The heat of summer
Brought intense
Emotion and depth

Of trust to
My life as I
Learned to love again.

As autumn falls
Time and distance
Cool the flames

And bring me to
A new place
Of sustained love.

Dagger

Forged by the fire
That awakened my heart,
The dagger was destined
To play its part.

Honed on the wheel
That turns our lives,
Made to be sharper
Than all other knives.

Wielded by hands
That meant only love
Each tiny nudge
Built to a shove.

Pushing our lives
Farther apart
And thrusting the dagger
Deep into my heart.

How?

How do I say good bye to
    A love that could never be?
How do I re-cage a heart
    That's newly been set free?

How can I not yearn
    To hear your voice each day?
How can I not see you
    And pretend that I'm okay?

How can I stop loving
    A man who is so dear?
How can I do this
    And never shed a tear?

How do I move on
    To something bold and new?
How do I forget
    How much I care for you?

Let Me In

I want to know
Your dreams and fears.
Let me in
To share the tears.

I want to be
Part of you life.
Let me in
To share the strife.

I want to learn
About your heart
Let me in
To the deepest part.

I want to care
And love you so.
Let me in
Your heart to know.

On Gossamer Wings

On gossamer wings
My spirit soars.
As I look
Into your eyes.

Love is a thing
I can not ignore,
As I glide
Here in the sky.

Soar high my heart
On these thin wings
Over mountains
Hills and streams.

'Til night departs
And morning sings
"He's only
In your dreams".

Stand

"I trust you with my life",
You said, as I took the
Key from your hand.

I wanted to say
"I trust you with my heart,"
But I could only stand

There, and say, "I know,"
When I wanted to tell
You, "I love you," and

To hold you, and
Take the pain away; but
I could only stand

There, then turn and
Walk away, holding
The key in my hand.

Why?

I want to know why you don't see
How much I love you; what you mean to me.

What is the matter with my loving you?
We've had a friendship that's seen us through

Twenty years of our lives, the good and the bad;
The best and the worst times that we've had.

Why can't you see that my love grew
Out of our friendship and all we've been through?

What have I done that's been so wrong?
It seems I've tried for oh so long

To show you how much I care.
But all you do is sit and stare.

Why can't you see that it is true?
All I want is to love you.

DEATH

Auction

"Sold!" he cries,
And then moves on
To the next item
Of the day.

"What am I bid for…."
What ever it is
He'll take whatever
You'll pay.

A nice little table,
A plate, a tool,
Some books, or
An antique fife.

What price can be put
On the things that are left
To be sold
At the end of a life.

Called to Freedom

A body too weak to work well.
A voice that fought each word.
But you listened with an open heart
Heeding the voice of the Lord.

"Come unto me", called the Lord,
"Your reward is Peace.
Freedom is yours again.
Rest now, in sweet release."

You are walking tall again,
A smile upon your face.
Your blue eyes shining bright
As you walk along in Grace.

You will be missed upon this Earth,
By family and by friends.
Our hearts will have an empty place,
Until we meet again.

A sad good bye and tears we shed,
As we send you on your way.
But we know we'll meet again,
When we come along one day.

Checkered Flag

The race is run,
The laps are done.
The checkered flag has waved.

The laps you've led,
You've won, they said,
It's off to victory lane.

The celebration has begun,
The long race you have run,
Has brought us here today.

Although your race is done,
We will celebrate your run,
Under the checkered flag.

Daddy's Boots

There are imprints
In the garage floor.
They are the tracks
Of my Daddy's boots.

I used to follow along
As he tilled the garden;
My feet dwarfed by the tracks
Of my Daddy's boots.

After his death,
His boots went to another.
There will be no more tracks
Of my Daddy's boots.

Firemen

Firemen aren't supposed to die.
They're supposed to live forever.
Fighting fires; saving lives;
Making our world better.

If ordained that he must fall
Lord, let it be in service.
For if he falls otherwise;
They'll say, "He doesn't deserve this."

"He's spent his life in service
To his community.
If he had to die, why
Not in the line of duty?"

The spark that gives us life,
The flame that lights our eyes,
Grows a little dimmer
Each time a fireman dies.

Forever 46

The fair-haired boy played football
    With his family on holidays.
He held to a faith which sustained
    The fighter on a far off island.
He found his place in history
    As the leader of the free world;
Facing the enemies of freedom
    With fearlessness.
Then fatal shots rang out; framed in a film;
    Flaying our innocence.
Followers flocked to see
    The end of the fairytale.
A son's farewell salute; a flame
    At the final resting place;
And in our hearts he is
    Forever forty-six.

Genie

Because of
Your love
Reaching out to
Others, we
Now know how to
Give of ourselves.
Everyone who knew you
Now grieves for you.
Even though we know
Where you are.
Even though we know
Eternal joy is yours. We
Keep thinking "He is gone".
So we grieve for our Brother,
      Uncle and Friend.

Heavenly Fish Fry

Heaven threw a fish fry
And invited you to come,
There's catfish, carp and crappie
And lots of little drum.

It's time to rest and eat your fill
Of heaven's hearty feast.
There's plenty here for everyone,
The greatest and the least.

On the banks of river Jordan
Put away your pole and line
On heaven's catch of perfect fish
Forever you will dine.

In Memory of Grandma

When I think of Grandma
I remember…
    Peanut butter by the spoonful.
    Christmas candy made with love.
    Homemade noodles that no one could match.
    Cold catfish on the back of the stove.

When I think of Grandma
I remember…
    Holiday meals when the house would not hold us all.
    Weekend night when the back room was wall to wall people.
    Games of Yatzee, Scrabble, and Blow-it.
    Jigsaw puzzles that she worked upside down while standing.

When I think of Grandma
I remember…
    Violets, Geraniums, Rose-moss and all other flowers.
    Pictures of all of us proudly displayed on walls and shelves.
    Crocheted afghans, dolls, hot pan holders, and washcloths.
    Birthdays that were special just because she was there.

When I think of Grandma
I remember…
    Soap operas that were watched daily.
    Taking her fishing at Dean Lake.
    Collecting rocks wherever she went.
    Her trying to teach me about "greens".

  When I think of Grandma
  I remember that she loved us all.

Ode to Mom

In Eighty-one years
You had quite a life;
Daughter, sister, aunt,
Mother and wife.

Oldest of ten
You mothered all;
When a child was in need
You answered the call.

You married your love
After World War Two
Life was not easy
But the love was true.

After years of waiting
A child you bore;
A single gift, though
You wished for more.

After forty years
Your husband died.
He left this world
But was still your guide.

You and your daughter
Traveled the states;
Fifteen in all afore
That fateful date.

A minor bruise
Upon your head
Too big inside
The doctors said.

Though it broke our hearts
We let you go.
You are free now
The Universe to know.

Of Death and Television

The little boy's
red eyes
searched
the preacher's
shocked
sad face
for
the answer
to
his innocent
question.

The little boy's
question was
"Why
can't my
friends
come back
alive?
When people
die
on TV
they
come back
alive
on another
show."

The Pianist

She played Boogie Woogie for the Grandkids,
And Onward Christian Soldiers for the church
Every time a pianist was needed
On that piano bench of hers she perched.

She played the songs note by note
Lifted up in joy and praise;
And we would all sing along
To the songs of gone by days.

Today she plays for Heaven's choir
The greatest music ever made;
And every time we hear the songs
We remember the music that she played.

Three Brothers

Once upon a
Sunny day
Three brothers went
Out to play.

"I want to skate,"
Said one to two;
"'Mr. Johnson's
Pond will do."

Down the hill
He ran so fast
The warning signs
He ran right past.

On the ice
Sliding out and back
He never saw
The telltale crack.

"Help," he cried
As he fell in.
His brothers ran
Their help to lend.

The life of one
Two could not save;
And all three boys
Went to their graves.

Once upon a
Sunny day
A town to rest
Three brothers lay.

Virgil

A baby lost hours after birth
Now unknown on this Earth.

His parents gone; no one can say
When he was born; on what day.

A name and a year on a stone,
The dates of his life still unknown.

Somewhere a record must be kept.
A baby died. His parents wept.

The search continues for his dates.
The record exists. It sits and waits.

The time will come. They will be known,
And finally etched on his stone.

You can't take it with you

There is no U-haul
    behind the hearse.
There is no room
    for treasure or purse.

Glories gathered on
    this Earth
In heaven will
    have no worth.

Shining gold and
    lovely gems
Will be useless
    when we see Him.

The treasures we
    have stored above
Grow not of Earth
    but of love.

IN BETWEEN

A Child Out of Time

The lullabies were
    Songs of war,
Tunes sung
    Twenty years before.

Beliefs in God and
    Country for life.
Attitudes born out
    Of strife.

A child born in
    A new war,
Things were different
    Than before.

Love of country
    Gone away,
But this child learned
    Every day,

Songs of war
    Still the rhyme,
To this child
    Born out of time.

Abandoned Boat

You are abandoned,
    Cold and alone,
    On the icy bank
    Of the North Grand River.

Tethered to a tall tree,
    You spend the winter
    Thinking only of spring.

When spring comes
    The water also
    Will come.

Rising fast, it will carry with it
    Trees that will take you
    Far from this place.

You will be tossed and tumbled,
    Ripped and torn,
    Smashed and splintered.

You will once again
    Wash onto a bank,
    Alone and broken now,

With only a memory
    Of what life once was
    For you;

When you carried
    A precious cargo
    Of human lives
    Across the river
    That destroyed you.

Dear Grandma

Dear Grandma Dobbins
You've had quite a life.
At twelve years old
You became a wife.

At thirteen, instead
Of childish fun,
You were having
Your first son.

Later, came sixteen
More babies to you;
Each one a blessing,
This is true.

Visited by tragedy
Over the years.
You've stood strong,
Against the tears.

Your progeny grew
And each went their own way.
Yet we gather together
Here today

Your kids and grandkids,
And their grandkids too,
All came here to say,
Happy 90th Birthday to you.

My Tribute to Bob Murry

You've touched the hearts of many
Young and old alike.

We will always love and honor you.
We'll be here as your dike.

You've touched the young by teaching them,
Just what it means to be,

Good and strong and loving,
To a very high degree.

You've taught the old through your life,
What children mean to you.

And many of them have turned around,
And now feel that way too.

You've taught me too,
I see it now,

To be a good person,
You helped me learn how.

In your eyes
I see the sorrow.

But you'll return
On the morrow.

We love you, Bob,
And always will,

For in our lives,
A void you fill.

Off the beaten path

Off the beaten path,
Far from a major trail,
Finding peace and solitude
That can not be found
Housed where others have
Etched a mark over time.
Beneath the feet lies
Earth that has yet to
Answer to man's footfalls.
The silence of the
Earth speaks of
New and different
Paths for all to walk.
Another will follow
Then no more will this be
Hallowed ground.

The Back Porch

I move slowly around the old Fort buildings,
and stop on the Factory's back porch.

The Fort is on a bluff, overlooking the Missouri River,
A site laid-out by Lewis and Clark.

I think of the time when these buildings were new,
and the troubles of the modern world seem to fade.

There were no power plants polluting the air,
and dodging autos to cross the road was unheard-of.

I see a squirrel playing along the river bank,
and a hawk swooping toward its resting place.

The trees rustle, bending low in the breeze,
and the water splashes against the muddy bank below.

These things calm me, and I know
that I'll soon return,
just to ease my mind.

The Journey

Fifty years ago
Two lives joined
Together to travel
Life's rugged path.

Through good times
And bad; through
Sickness and health
They traveled together.

Now there is one
Left alone to travel
That path to its
Final destination.

Alone, yet not.
For he still walks
Within her heart.
Forever together.

The River

The river is the history
Of the pioneer and is home.

The river is the foundation
Where future generations shall roam.

The river is so beautiful
Its banks covered with flowers.

The river is a world, alone,
Much different than ours.

The Tumor

About the size of a lemon, and white,
    Like the walls of the room where he lay.

The room was cold, like the October air,
    But the tumor was in a warm pink lung.

The air grew cooler as the seventy year old man
    Heard the doctor's conclusion.

He only has six weeks to live; he might not see the first snow;
    He wouldn't see spring with out surgery.

Two days later the tumor was in a sealed container of gelatin,
    Awaiting shipment to the lab.

The man's body lay in another cool room;
    A wheezing, gurgling machine breathed for him.

Three weeks later, the man left the cool hospital room,
    The warm light of life again shining in his eyes.

He lay in bed at home for the next three months,
    A hot machine pumped cold oxygen into his
    warm body.

In February, he remembered the doctor who said
    That he could not raise a garden again.

In March, he began to plant his garden
    With little help from his oxygen machine.

Thunder Ridge

There's a church upon the hill
Just across the bridge.
A white frame building, small and neat;
Folks call it Thunder Ridge.

The preacher man is new in town;
Don't know where from he came.
But since he's been in these here parts
Things just ain't the same.

He speaks with love and tenderness
As he looks upon the crowd.
Yet when he sees a sinner's face
He just cries out loud.

Lightning flashes in his eyes,
And tears just fall like rain.
The people know that there's no chance
For this sin to remain.

He holds his Bible in the air
Then he brings it down
With such a crashing blow
That thunder shakes the town.

Ever seat in the church
Is filled each Sunday morn.
And everyone in this town
Has newly been reborn.

Thunder rolls now and then
From high on Thunder Ridge;
But we're all trying, oh so hard,
To cross that Holy Bridge.

Tight Rope

I walk a tight rope
With out a net.
No crowd to cheer,
Or mourn my death.

I walk alone
Above the ground,
My beating heart
The only sound.

One wrong step
And down I go.
No one else
Will ever know

How many steps
I had left
To cross the wire
With out a net.

Timing

From our point of view
      It's not the time or place.
But we have been brought here
      By the Lord's amazing Grace.

Placed in this situation
      To deal with what we face;
Timing is of the essence when
      Running the human race.

The time that we are given,
      Like sand in a vase,
Put there by Holy Hands,
      Is not ours to waste.

It may not be the time
      That we wish for this place,
But to let it pass us by
      Would surely be disgrace.

We Won

The day is long, the day is hard
And we've only just begun.

The director says that we can win;
But there is no prize offered.

What we will win is in our hearts,
And in the hearts of others.

There are children here
Who have not seen
A band march as we will.

They will watch
And they will see
The pride that fills the air
As the band goes marching by,
The joy that we will share.

We won today
No trophy greater,
Than that which we have won;
The praise and respect of the children,
The joy of the young.

SMILES

A Cat's Day

The black cat
Chased a rat.
She caught a mouse
In the house.
Was that a bird
That she heard?
She saw a fish
In a dish.
In a cap
She took a nap.
What a day!
It's fun to play.

Candle Poem

Sweet candle light,
Burn so bright,
Show us the way
Through the night.

As you glow,
Love you show,
Precious light
Peace to know.

Fall

Leaves skip merrily
    Down the lane.
Wind dances with
    The weather vane.
Apples bend the
    Tree limbs down.
Corn in the field
    Is turning brown.
Geese fly south
    Away from snow;
And spider webs
    Begin to grow.
Fall is here
    It's safe to say,
So winter can't be
    Far away.

His Majesty

His Majesty sits
High in a tree;
He is master of all
That he can see.

White crown shining
Against an azure sky
He watches his world
As it passes by.

Falling fast
He dives from the tree
And soars in all
His majesty.

Poetry in Motion

Hands move to an
    Unheard rhythm.
Face lightens and darkens
    To the mood of a song.
Words flow silently
    From one to another.
Poetry in motion, silent
    Language, American Sign.

Sky Pictures

I see a lamb's head
Way up high.
There goes a puppy
Floating by.
I see a clown
With a big nose,
And funny hair.
There it goes.
People and animals
In the sky;
All seen with
Imaginative eyes.

Summer Sunset

Evening sun
Kissed orange
By hazy
Summer sky.

Clouds squeeze
Jagged teeth
Into skin.

Man sips
Sweet drops
From summer sun.

Windy Day

Trees lean one to another
Passing secret messages.

They bow down, paying
Homage to Mother Earth.

Leaves scurry across roads
Chased by unseen foes.

Seeds ripped from their birthplaces
Take flight seeking new homes.

Words of Wisdom

Dream a dream
    It will come true.
Wish and wishes
    Come to you.

Hope breeds hope,
    As you will find.
Love brings love
    From all mankind.

With these four words,
    The world is yours.
Use them to open
    Life's closed doors.

Printed in the United States
141269LV00002B/97/P